Mr. Tickle
WO

Inspired by life with the Little Misses
Illustrated by Adam Hargreaves

What was intended as harmless advice by you will be taken as a supreme insult by them.

Little Miss Greedy   **Mr. Skinny**

**There is only one
answer to the question:
'Does my bum look big in this?'**

Little Miss Splendid

Mr. Brave

Never watch football with a woman, unless you want to talk about who's got the nicest legs.

Little Miss
Dotty

Mr. Grumpy

Women like a show of public affection from their men. Try holding hands.

Mr. Tickle

What to do if you forget a woman's birthday: Leave.

Little Miss Bossy

Never mix women, maps and confined spaces.

**No woman will ever be
'ready in a minute'.**

Little Miss Late

D.I.Y. shops are best avoided when buying a gift.

Mr. Dizzy   **Little Miss Star**

Having no idea what you've done wrong is a perfectly normal state of affairs.

To avoid being late for work, get to the bathroom first.

Little Miss Splendid

Mr. Rush

No matter what they tell you, nobody needs 17 pairs of shoes.

Little Miss Splendid   Mr. Small

**Never, ever look in
a woman's handbag.**

Mr. Brave

When women are on a diet,
the food on your plate doesn't
seem to count.

Mr. Greedy   **Little Miss Star**

For a 2 week holiday they'll pack for 6 months, and then expect you to carry it.

Mr. Skinny

**Women have two weapons:
tears and cosmetics.**

Only women see the difference between beige, off-white and eggshell.

**Women think wallets
are for sharing.**

Little Miss Bossy   **Mr. Strong**

A woman has the last word in any argument. Anything a man says after that is the beginning of a new argument.

Mr. Grumpy   **Little Miss Stubborn**

Men wake up as good-looking
as they went to bed.
Women somehow deteriorate
during the night.

Mr. Perfect

**Little Miss
Splendid**

Most women have an average
of 237 items in their bathroom.
A man would not be able to
identify most of these items.

Mr. Nosey

Women lie when they say
they are happy for you to go out
and play golf . . . as you will
discover when you get back
home after playing golf.

Little Miss Bossy   **Mr. Strong**

Invite your most badly behaved mate round – you'll look a saint in comparison.

Mr. Messy

You can be sure that her friends will know everything about you.

Mr. Quiet   **Little Miss**   **Little Miss**
                    Chatterbox   **Giggles**

If you're looking for Miss Right, just make sure her first name isn't Always.

Little Miss Wise

If something you say can be interpreted in 2 ways, you can guarantee she will jump to the wrong one.

Little Miss Quick

She'll use your razor
when hers is blunt.
Now yours is.

Mr. Fussy

Women will spend £60
on a haircut that would have
cost a man £8. It is therefore best
to say on a regular basis
'Ooh, had your hair done?'

Mr. Perfect   **Little Miss Star**

**A woman's mind is
cleaner than a man's.
She changes it more often.**

Little Miss Fickle

A woman will go on holiday with a girlfriend for two weeks, and then come home, call the same girlfriend and talk for three hours.

Little Miss Chatterbox

Women never have anything to wear.

Little Miss Late

Always compromise: on your part admit you were wrong and apologise. And then on her part she will forgive you . . .

Mr. Wrong

**Little Miss
Stubborn**

. . . **probably.**